Contents

Dúchas The Heritage Service

An Roinn Comhshaoil agus Rialtais Áitiúil
Department of the Environment and Local Government

© 2002

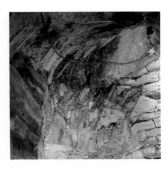

Introduction

The great stone castles, which still stand in the countryside and in towns such as Trim, are potent symbols of the Norman occupation of Ireland. These castles were the main strategy used by the Normans to consolidate their territorial gains as they spread outwards from their initial landings in the south east of the country.

Background: Interior of the Barbican Gate by George Dunoyer, 1859.
Courtesy: Royal Society of Antiquaries of Ireland.

Introduction

Trim Castle was built during the late 12th and 13th centuries. It overlooks a crossing on the River Boyne and dominates the town that grew up around it. The great stone keep, built by Hugh de Lacy (d.1186) and his son Walter (1168-1241), forms the centrepiece of this imposing fortress. Two important gatehouses, several defensive towers and the remains of several other notable buildings are contained within the curtain walls that enclose over 1.5 hectares of land, making Trim the largest castle in the country.

During the 13th and 14th centuries, it served as the principal residence and centre of administration for the Lords of Meath. By the 15th century, Trim Castle had been absorbed into the royal estates and was placed in the care of a succession of constables or other officials. As a peripheral Castle of the Crown, Trim suffered neglect with only occasional works and repairs. During the 17th century, then semi-ruinous, Trim Castle was once again besieged for a brief period by the Royalist forces and eventually served as a Cromwellian stronghold. Later in that century the castle was again repaired in anticipation of the forthcoming fray between James II and William III. By the 18th century Trim Castle was abandoned and fell into a ruinous state and remained a picturesque site popular with visiting antiquarians and artists. Ownership had passed through various families until it was finally purchased by the State from Lord Dunsany in 1993. It is now managed by Dúchas The Heritage Service of the Department of the Environment and Local Government.

(1)	The Ditch of the Ringwork Castle	(8)	The Moat
(2)	The Keep	(9)	The Trim Gate
(3)	The Forebuildings	(10)	The Prison
(4)	The Great Hall	(11)	The Barbican Gate
(5)	The Solar	(12)	The Bailey
(6)	The River Gate	(13)	The Mint
(7)	The Curtain Walls		

History

The Coming of the Normans

When Henry II, the first Plantagenet King of England, came to Ireland in 1171, a few years after the original Norman incursions, it was to curb the expansionist ambitions of his barons. Henry feared particularly that Richard de Clare, Earl of Pembroke, known as Strongbow, might set up an independent Anglo-Norman kingdom in Ireland. In the king's train was Hugh de Lacy, Lord of Weobley, owner of large estates and many stone castles in England. Henry granted de Lacy the ancient Irish kingdom of Midhe, which included the modern county of Meath, and appointed him Justiciar of Ireland. By granting these lands to de Lacy, the king blocked the northward progress of Strongbow, who, with his Irish allies, had already conquered all of Leinster.

Soon after his arrival at Trim, de Lacy began the first phase of fortification by building a wooden defensive fort, encircled by a trench and enclosed within a wooden stockade, a spiked enclosure, at the highest point on the site overlooking the River Boyne.

Archaeological excavations have revealed evidence of occupation and settlement of the castle site spanning a considerable period of time. The discovery of Neolithic flints indicates human presence in prehistoric times although no traces of dwellings from this period were uncovered. Settlements of the early medieval period were discovered including a corn-drying kiln, a post and wattle house and an animal stockade along with other buildings which stood within an 8th / 9th century enclosure. These may have been the remains of a farm or grange associated with the monastery of Trim since documents from the 14th century suggest that the land was formerly the property of the church.

Henry II from Topographia Hiberniae. Giraldus Cambrensis, 1185, copied c. 1200. Courtesy: National Library of Ireland.

Trim Castle looking across the River Boyne.

History

The First Castle

Hugh de Lacy's first castle, termed a Ringwork Castle, is vividly described in a contemporary Norman French poem, "the Song of Dermot and the Earl". Translated from medieval French, the poem states:-

> Then Hugh de Lacy
> Fortified a house at Trim
> And dug a ditch around it
> And enclosed it within a stockade
> Within the house he then placed
> Great Knights and Barons

The post-holes and trenches of the stockade were uncovered during the archaeological investigations along the northern perimeter of the enclosure. Inside, in the north west quadrant, archaeologists discovered the burnt remains of a well-stocked granary. To the south, are the footings of a rectangular stone building. With its east-west orientation, the suggestion is that this was a chapel. There were other buildings in this area; timber-framed structures on dry-stone footings with rough stone-paved floors and central hearths. These probably served as dwellings, but the location of the former principal residence is unclear.

The high status residence of a 12th century ringwork castle should be a tower or a hall house, constructed in either wood or stone. The strong stone footings in the north east quadrant suggest that the latter, a residential hall over a vaulted cellar, was built at Trim. The keep soon replaced this and the lower fabric of the house was incorporated into the 13th century fore-buildings of the keep. The enclosed space was no doubt well-utilised, with houses, workshops, stores, and animal shelters. Outside the ringwork, the hill was enclosed within a wooden palisade fence forming a "bailey"; a protected area for houses, animal pens and small gardens, and the work yards of masons and carpenters. Post holes and stone hearths, the remains of some of these houses, were unearthed

A Conjectural View of the 12th Century Ringwork Castle

1	Early Gate House (Trim Gate)
2	Inner Pallisade
3	Granary
4	Stone House
5	Ditch of the Ringwork Castle
6	St. Mary's Abbey
7	River Boyne

History

Hugh de Lacy. From Expugnatio Hibernica. Giraldus Cambrensis, 1189. Courtesy: National Library of Ireland.

during the excavation. The discovery of the footings of an early wooden gatehouse on the site of the northwest (Trim) Gate indicates the strong defensive nature and the extent of the first ringwork castle and bailey.

The town that grew up around the castle takes it name, *Ath Troim*, [the ford of the Elder trees] from an ancient secular and ecclesiastical settlement, which can be traced back to before 900 AD. It is known that, in the opening decades of the 12th century, Trim was associated with a local ruling dynasty, the *Uí Chaindelbáin*, and may have been the site of their principal residence.

Hugh de Lacy

Giraldus Cambrensis (Gerald of Wales), a younger son of the Anglo-Norman De Barri family of South Wales, priest and chaplain to Henry II, made two visits to Ireland, the first when he accompanied Prince John in 1186. In his *Expugnatio Hibernica* (The Conquest of Ireland) which he completed in 1187, he introduces us to many of the personalities of the Norman conquest of Ireland.

Of Hugh de Lacy he writes: -

"If you wish to know what Hugh's complexion and features were like, he was dark with dark sunken eyes and flattened nostrils. His face was grossly disfigured down the right side as far as his chin by a burn, the result of an accident."

Giraldus describes a reliable sober Frenchman, well versed in the business of war. However, apparently his personality changed after the death of his first wife and he became lustful, greedy and more ambitious for his own advancement than was proper.

Hugh de Lacy was the great grandson of Walter de Lacy, a knight of Lassy in the Calvados region of Normandy, who followed the military household of William fitzOsbern in the invasion of England led by William the Conqueror in 1066. Walter was granted vast estates between the River Severn and the mountains of Wales, the Welsh Marches, which he then secured with many strong castles. The fitzOsberns lost their English lands following an unsuccessful rebellion against the King and Walter became the chief tenant of the Crown, building a castle befitting his status at Ludlow.

Roger de Lacy succeeded his father in 1085. After unsuccessful rebellions against William II, Roger was exiled and Ludlow and its baronies passed to his brother Hugh. On his death in 1115, Henry I ordered that the lands pass to Sybil, the daughter or possibly a niece of Hugh. The order also stipulated that she marry Henry's loyal and ambitious servant Payn fitzJohn.

In the disorder that followed Henry's death and Stephen's accession to the throne, England was rife with dispute and rebellion and many of the Norman barons supported the rival claim to the throne of Henry's daughter, Matilda. When fitzJohn was killed in 1137, Stephen acted quickly to control the Welsh marches and ordered the marriage of Sybil to Joce de Dinan, one of his knights.

A 12th century chronicler described the state of the English countryside,

"Every rich man burdened the unfortunate country Folk with work at their castles. When they finished building them they filled them with devils and bad men"

History

From Normandy, Roger's son, Gilbert, undertook a long campaign to recapture his English inheritance. By 1150, with the help of other disaffected tenants, he succeeded in taking Ludlow and, by 1155, after the accession of Henry II, he regained much of the de Lacy baronies. Gilbert, his eldest son, Robert, and many of his former rival kinsmen set out on crusade in 1159, and were not heard of again.

In 1165, Gilbert's younger son, Hugh, took charge at Ludlow and was active with Henry II in his military campaigns in Wales. When he came to Ireland with Henry in 1171-1172, he was made Lord of Meath, constable of Dublin and Justiciar of Ireland. The vast Irish estates that he acquired put Hugh de Lacy and his descendants at the centre of Anglo-Norman affairs in Ireland. However, in the period between 1172 and 1186, Hugh was to spend less than ten years in Ireland. For the brief period before he was summoned, with many of his barons, to serve in Henry II's war in France in 1173, Hugh's army crossed Meath, living off the spoils of their raids. His expertise and experience in warfare gained with Henry in Wales was put into practice, particularly along the western boundaries with Connacht and the northern boundaries with Breifne (Cavan) with its difficult terrain of lakes and hills.

A strange account of one raid is given to us by Giraldus.

"Hugh de Lacy with his army, passed a night at Fore. He made his soldiers restore all the corn which they had taken from the churches and the mill, except for a small quantity of oats taken from the mill which two soldiers had kept and put before their horses. One of these horses went mad in the night and dashed out his brains. In the morning when the master of the other horse was jeering his companions for restoring the corn he suddenly fell dead at the side of Hugh de Lacy."

History

At strategic places Hugh left garrisons in quickly assembled wooden castles built on strong earthworks. The area within his control was then subdivided among his barons who, in turn, built their own castles and consolidated their conquest in a manner unequalled in Ireland.

On his departure for France in 1173, De Lacy's occupation of Meath was incomplete and the garrison at Trim was small. Hugh Tyrell was left as custodian. Ruardhi O'Connor, King of Connacht, who had claims on the ancient kingdom, attacked Meath and, finding *"all the castles there empty and deserted"*, he burned the abandoned castles including Trim. The poem "the Song of Dermot and the Earl" continues,

> They demolished the motte
> And razed everything to the ground
> But first they burned down the castle

However, the Norman armies of Leinster under Strongbow's lieutenant, Raymond le Gros, expelled O`Connor's army, allowing Hugh Tyrell to return and repair the castles of Meath.

> Hugh Tyrell returned to Trim
> Restored his fortress
> And guarded it with honor
> Until the return of his lord

A Typical Motte and Bailey Castle

History

When de Lacy returned in 1175, the conquest of Meath began in earnest. Work began on the stone keep at Trim, and he also established other strong castles including one at Drogheda, the port town situated at the mouth of the River Boyne. Elsewhere in his Lordship, a territory that extended from the Shannon to the Irish Sea, motte and bailey castles were built close to existing Irish settlements and guarding roadways and river crossings.

De Lacy introduced a new feudal order. Every aspect of life, from religion to trade and even hunting and fishing was now controlled. Trim became the hub for this transformation, at the head of a system designed to exploit these fertile lands; for the lordship of Meath was rich in natural attributes of forest, river and lake, with access to the sea through the protected port of Drogheda.

Even today, the landscape of the area provides a fascinating physical archive of the activities of the De Lacys and their companions. Archaeological remains, in the form of a dense network of earthwork castles, sites of manor houses enclosed by moats, abbeys, churches, boroughs, mills, bridges and weirs, are abundant. The extensive ruins of Newtown Trim, which date from the 13th and 14th centuries, are a fine example of Norman settlement. These remains bear testament to an era of prosperity that existed in the lordship; brought about by dramatic changes in agricultural practices through extensive tillage and the creation of field systems for stock management. The lands were far more valuable than any the de Lacy family had held up to now and the rents and tolls from them provided funds for the building of Trim Castle.

At Trim, work on the construction of the great stone keep forged ahead. Of unique design, on the plan of a Greek cross, the keep was built in three phases during the years 1175-1205.

The Cathedral of Saints Peter and Paul, Newtown.
Gabriel Beringer (1773).
Courtesy: National Library of Ireland.

15

History

Hugh's achievements in Ireland were those of a successful conqueror and his commitment and organisational abilities are recounted in the contemporary histories and documented by Giraldus, who reported to Henry II. As guardian of Dublin, Hugh made grants of land on which castles were built, and as chief governor of Ireland between 1177-1181 he fortified Leinster with many castles. His enthusiasm and ambition alarmed the King and when Hugh married O'Connor's daughter *"in the manner of that country"* (Giraldus), the King's concerns were confirmed. Henry took steps to curb Hugh's ambition, and prepared the young Prince John to take charge as Lord of Ireland.

Prince John's army travelled to Ireland in 1185 and marched through Leinster and Munster, making land grants to new tenants and establishing some order in colonising these territories. Hugh de Lacy reluctantly accompanied John on this expedition, while his own barons strengthened their hold in the western part of Meath and well beyond the boundaries of his lordship.

In 1186, Hugh resumed control of his dominions. While inspecting work in his castle on the site of the ancient monastery of Durrow, an Irish follower Gilla-gan-inathair na Midhe stuck Hugh and killed him instantly. Some accounts suggest that it was in revenge for the death of his brother at Loughsewedy and others say it was in anger for the desecration of the monastery of St. Columcille.

Walter de Lacy

Seal of Walter de Lacy

Because his son, Walter, was under age at the time of Hugh's death, Trim and all of the de Lacy lands and their incomes were escheated (claimed) by the Crown. Only when Walter was 21, in 1189, did he succeed to his lands in both England and Ireland. By 1194, Walter had joined with John de Courcy in attacking the lands of Prince John who was in rebellion against his brother, King Richard. When peace was restored between the royal brothers, Walter was deprived of his lands until he agreed to pay 3100 marks in return for the king's benevolence. Walter then served with Richard in France until the death of the king in 1199. Walter returned to England with King John in 1200 who, soon after, arranged the marriage of Walter to Margaret de Braose, the daughter of one of the king's closest confidants. Throughout this period, royal officials administered the De Lacy estates. In 1201, Walter returned to Ireland. His father-in-law, William de Braose, held Ludlow on behalf of the King until 1207 when Walter de Lacy and King John finally made their peace. By 1208 William de Braose himself was in conflict with the king, and took refuge with Walter in Ireland.

The structure of the government in Ireland was weak because of the disparate Norman and Irish factions and consequently in 1210, King John mounted an expedition to Ireland. Landing at Waterford, John marched towards Dublin where Walter was preparing to seek terms. Instead, John received the submission of de Lacy's tenants against Walter and moved on with his vast entourage and swollen armies of loyal supporters to camp for two nights at Trim. Walter, his brother Hugh, together with William de Braose were forced to flee to France. As part of a general reconciliation between the king and his barons in 1214, Walter came to an agreement with John and his estates .were restored.

Silver penny minted in Dublin in the reign of King John.

17

History

Three major events took place in the following years that kept Walter away from Ireland. King John died in 1216, civil war broke out in England, followed by an invasion of French Barons. De Lacy, as a member of the Regency Council governing the country, would have been deeply involved in these events. His arrival back in Ireland in 1220 was recorded in the Annals of the Four Masters. De Lacy seems to have launched a new campaign of attempted conquest of counties Cavan and Leitrim, where he and some of his lieutenants were engaged expanding the Meath lordship.

After another brief visit to England in 1223, Walter was ordered to return to Ireland where his brothers, Hugh and William, were in rebellion. Trim Castle was by now a substantial structure and Walter had to undertake a seven-week siege in order to retrieve his property and bring Meath to obedience. Having given his word to the King that he would suppress the rebels in Meath and elsewhere, he pledged his castles at Ludlow and Trim to his royal master for a period of two years. An important description of Trim Castle from 1224 survives. It lists a hall, *[aulum]*, house *[domus]* and chambers *[camera]*. Walter's position in Trim was now relatively secure. However, in 1228 it was discovered that he had not paid all of the fines due to the Crown for the previous twenty years. In a compromise, Henry III agreed to allow Walter to remain in possession of Trim but he was left in serious debt to the Crown and to his financiers.

Walter de Lacy *"the most eminent of the nobles of Ireland"* (Matthew Paris) died in 1241 outliving his son Gilbert (d. 1230) and his grandson Walter (d. 1238). His burdened properties and *"wasted estates"* were returned to the Crown, before ultimately being divided between his two granddaughters, Matilda (Maud) and Margery (Margaret). Matilda was granted Trim Castle and half of the de Lacy estates in 1254.

History

The Mortimers

Trim Castle was to remain in the hands of the Mortimer family for 120 years. During that time the Mortimers, holding vast estates of lands in both Ireland and England, advanced through the ranks of the English aristocracy. Successive generations of the family occupied high positions and enjoyed favour at court, occupying a position just below that of royal dukes.

The first member of the family to hold Trim was Roger Mortimer, Lord of Wigmore, 1st Earl of March. At the time of his marriage to Joan de Geneville, Roger was already a dominant landowner in Ireland, holding the lordship of Dunamase in Laois through his share of the inheritance of the Marshall lordship of Leinster.

In 1308, Joan and Roger travelled to Ireland to take possession of their inheritance. It seems that on that occasion Mortimer wisely spent money on fortifying Trim Castle, probably as a defensive measure against the extended de Lacy family in Meath who would have seen him as an interloper. After a brief period abroad in France and Wales, Mortimer returned hastily to Ireland in 1315 and took the field at Kells in Co. Meath where he was defeated by the invading Scottish army of Edward Bruce who had the support of the de Lacys. Mortimer escaped capture and his deputy Walter Cusacke held out in Trim Castle. By the spring of 1317, as the King's Lieutenant, he returned to Ireland and forced the Scots and the de Lacys to retreat.

Trim was taken into royal care during the period when Mortimer was in dispute with Edward II and, later, when he was imprisoned in the Tower of London on a charge of treason, his lands and castles were declared forfeit.

History

Roger escaped from the Tower and fled to France and on his return to England in 1327 with his mistress, Queen Isabella, overthrew Edward II. Mortimer recovered Trim and the rest of his estates but three years later overweening ambition led him to his ignominious execution at Tyburn and most of the Mortimer properties were declared forfeit to the Crown. His widow, Joan surrendered Trim Castle in 1332, although it was returned to her briefly in 1337 and again in 1343 or 1344. In 1347 she was styled Countess of March and Lady of Trim although at this time she retired in favour of her grandson Roger Mortimer, as her son Edmund had died in 1331. Joan may have spent some part of her retirement in Trim during the difficult years of the 'Black Death' until she died, aged seventy, in 1356.

Roger Mortimer and Queen Isabella.
Courtsey: British Library.

The Mortimers

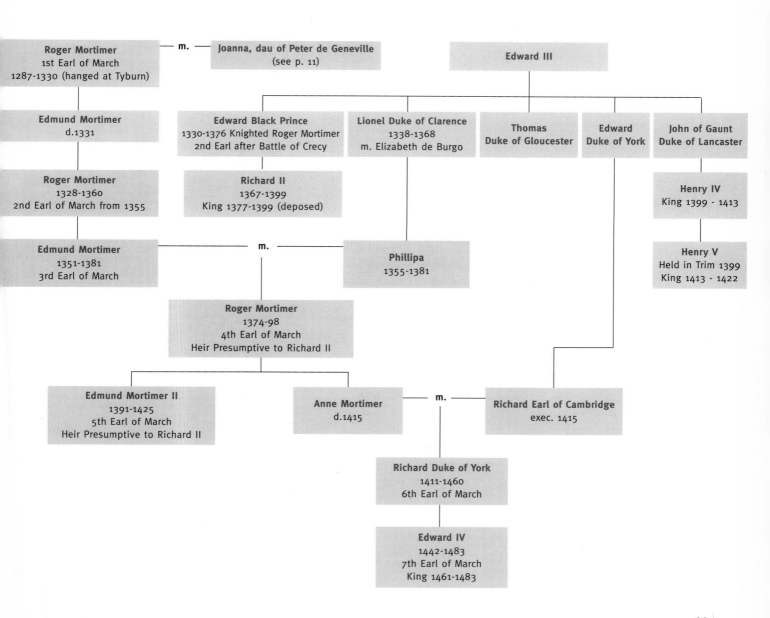

Roger Mortimer
1st Earl of March
1287-1330 (hanged at Tyburn)

m.

Joanna, dau of Peter de Geneville
(see p. 11)

Edward III

Edmund Mortimer
d.1331

Edward Black Prince
1330-1376 Knighted Roger Mortimer
2nd Earl after Battle of Crecy

Lionel Duke of Clarence
1338-1368
m. Elizabeth de Burgo

Thomas
Duke of Gloucester

Edward
Duke of York

John of Gaunt
Duke of Lancaster

Roger Mortimer
1328-1360
2nd Earl of March from 1355

Richard II
1367-1399
King 1377-1399 (deposed)

Henry IV
King 1399 - 1413

Edmund Mortimer
1351-1381
3rd Earl of March

m.

Phillipa
1355-1381

Henry V
Held in Trim 1399
King 1413 - 1422

Roger Mortimer
1374-98
4th Earl of March
Heir Presumptive to Richard II

Edmund Mortimer II
1391-1425
5th Earl of March
Heir Presumptive to Richard II

Anne Mortimer
d.1415

m.

Richard Earl of Cambridge
exec. 1415

Richard Duke of York
1411-1460
6th Earl of March

Edward IV
1442-1483
7th Earl of March
King 1461-1483

History

Roger Mortimer (1328-60), 2nd Earl of March was rewarded for his military service to Edward III particularly at the battle of Crecy (France) in 1346. He became a powerful figure at court and one of the original Knights of the Garter. Roger may never have visited Trim, however he did appoint one Cornelius Obruyn, to maintain a troop of 24 foot soldiers to look after his tenants and farmers on his manor at Trim. As constable of the English forces invading France, Mortimer died suddenly in February 1360, leaving an eight-year old son, Edmund as his heir.

As the young Edmund Mortimer (1351/2-81), 3rd Earl of March, was a minor, his inheritance, including Trim Castle, was taken into royal hands. A cousin, another Roger Mortimer, was appointed to the office of constable of Trim Castle for a brief period. A succession of constables followed, as the castle continued to function as a prison. In 1362, Art MacMurrough and his tanaiste were held prisoner there. During this period of royal custody of Trim, a major expedition led by the King Edward III's son Lionel, Duke of Clarence, visited Ireland. Lionel is known to have resided at Trim at intervals between the years 1362-65. Repair work was carried out at the castle during 1364-5 and, two years later, the great hall was rebuilt. These repairs were probably carried out in anticipation of the coming to Trim of Edmund Mortimer and his young bride, Philippa (1355-78), daughter and heir to Lionel, Duke of Clarence.

Roger Mortimer, 2nd Earl of March, Knight of the Garter.
Courtsey: British Library.

History

Edmund Mortimer was a considerable figure of his time, he held lands in both England and Wales and his revenues were probably surpassed by few, other than the king's sons, Edward, Prince of Wales and John of Gaunt, Duke of Lancaster. In Ireland, where he also held in his wife's right the Earldom of Ulster, the Lordship of Connacht and the vast estates attached, he was the most powerful landholder in the country. Even with such huge responsibilities in Ireland, Edmund Mortimer spent long periods away fighting the King's war in France and involved with affairs of state in England. He had visited Trim and held court there in July 1372, but it was not until May 1380 that he returned to Ireland as Lieutenant to the new king, Richard II. A year later he was dead from an illness contracted while campaigning in Munster.

When Edmund died, his son Roger was still a minor. During the next 12 years of royal care, the position of constable of the castle at Trim was held by John Reigne, whom Roger's father had appointed to the post for life.

Roger Mortimer, 4th Earl of March (1374-98), received his Irish estates in 1393. The Mortimers had continued their advance through the ranks of English aristocracy and Richard II had nominated Roger, because of family links, heir presumptive to the throne. With his huge wealth and vast estates in Ireland and England and his new position as Richard's named successor, Roger Mortimer was the most powerful noble of his lineage. He accompanied King Richard on his expedition to Ireland in 1394 and remained behind in the country after the King's departure for England the following year. Once settled at Trim, Roger obtained a licence to impose tolls on all goods entering several of the towns under his control, including Trim. He used the tolls for the purpose of, *'surrounding the town of Trim with a stone wall, paving it anew, improving the town, and in repressing the adjacent enemies and rebels'*. During the remaining four years of his life, Mortimer stayed in Ireland and lodged mainly at Trim Castle where he held court. He was killed in a skirmish at Kells, Co. Meath in 1398.

History

Edmund Mortimer 5th Earl of March was just six years old on the death of his father and yet again Mortimer lands including the castle of Trim were taken into royal care.

In 1399, Richard had been deposed by a Lancastrian coup followed by the accession of Henry IV. Prior to being deposed, Richard had taken refuge in Ireland and had left behind as hostages, Henry IV's son, Prince Hal, the future Henry V, and Humphrey, son of the Earl of Gloucester in Trim Castle. Edmund Mortimer's position was very precarious because he had become the recognised heir to Richard II on the death of his father. For many years he was seen as a threat to the Lancastrian regime and his lands were not restored to him until Henry V ascended the throne. The castle at Trim had been severely neglected during the twenty five-year period that it was held by Lancastrian royal officials and even the gaol at the castle was run-down.

Edmund Mortimer came to Ireland as the King's Lieutenant in 1424. However, his stay was short lived, having held Christmas court at Trim that year and received submissions from all the leading chiefs of Ulster, he died of the plague on January 18th 1425. The direct male line of the Mortimers ended with his death.

Later Centuries

It is unlikely that Edmund had had the time to commence any major refurbishment of Trim and within days of his death, the break up of his vast estates and a more serious decline of the castle had begun. Richard of York who inherited the estates, including Trim Castle and the liberty of Trim was the son of Edmund Mortimer's sister, Anne. Richard was a minor and so a succession of constables was appointed to oversee the property on behalf of the Crown. During his ownership it is likely that the decline of the once splendid royal castle and grand residence continued.

The Barbican Gate

History

It was not until 1449 that Richard of York arrived in Ireland as Lord Lieutenant, remaining in the country until the end of the following summer. It is likely that Richard carried out work on the fortifications of Trim so as to use the castle as a bolthole since civil war in England, the so-called Wars of the Roses, threatened. During the ensuing strife, Richard did indeed flee to Ireland, after his defeat at Ludford Bridge. He effectively set up a Yorkist administration in the country and held Parliament at Drogheda in February 1460. One of its provisions was that a distinctive coinage should be issued, and that there should be two mints, one each in the castles of Dublin and Trim; the main bastions of Yorkist power. That same year Richard returned to England but was killed at the battle of Wakefield. In March the following year, his son, Edward was victorious at Towton and was proclaimed King Edward IV. One of his first Irish acts was to appoint a comptroller of the mints and in 1461, Germyn Lynch of London, goldsmith, was appointed *'warden and master worker of our monies and coignes within our Castell of Dyvelyn [Dublin] and Trym'*.

Trim Castle by Rev. Samuel Wynne c. 1790

History

Once Trim Castle had been absorbed into the royal estates, a succession of constables was appointed to oversee the property that was still regarded as a symbol of royal power.

In 1524, Gerald, Earl of Kildare as Lord Deputy was ordered to repair the king's castles of Dublin and Trim. During the Kildare rebellion in December 1534, Trim was taken by Thomas Fitzgerald, son of Gerald, but he was easily driven from the castle by the following January. A strong garrison was installed and plans were made to have Trim refurbished as the Viceregal residence. Some repairs and new structural additions were carried out on the castle site but nothing of note has survived from that phase of building. On several occasions throughout the 16th century the idea of using Trim Castle to house the Lord Deputy was suggested but no major refurbishment was undertaken and the importance of Trim continued to decline as its buildings fell into disrepair. Following the Cromwellian wars, in the mid 17th century, when the castle was in the ownership of Sir Adam Loftus, soldiers and inhabitants of the town of Trim pillaged the castle and carried away planks, roof beams and lead.

Some minor repairs were carried out at the time of the Williamite wars but after that Trim Castle was allowed to fall into a ruinous state. During the 18th and early 19th centuries the picturesque ruin was owned by the Wellesleys, until the Marquis of Wellesley, elder brother of the Duke of Wellington sold his Irish estates in 1816. The castle was described in the sale catalogue in the following terms;

> 'The ancient grand structure, King John's Castle, one of the most superb ruins of the kingdom situated on the banks of the river Boyne. The principal part surrounded by the old walls, the castle yard, &c'.

The castle was purchased by Colonel Leslie of Glaslough, Co. Monaghan, whose son sold it in 1859 to his relatives, the Plunketts of Dunsany Castle. It was finally purchased by the State from Lord Dunsany in 1993 and is now conserved and managed by Dúchas The Heritage Service of the Department of the Environment and Local Government.

Floor Plans of the Keep

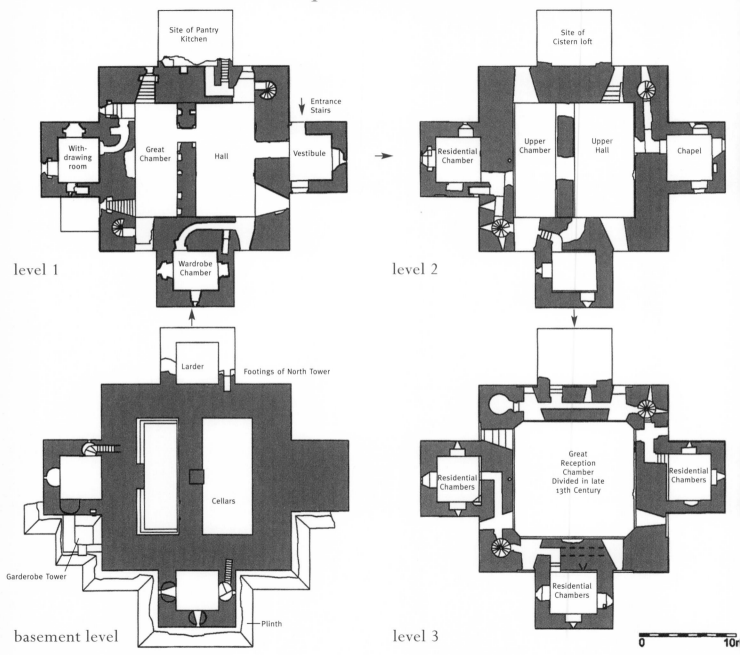

level 1

Site of Pantry Kitchen

With-drawing room

Great Chamber

Hall

Vestibule

Entrance Stairs

Wardrobe Chamber

basement level

Larder

Footings of North Tower

Cellars

Garderobe Tower

Plinth

level 2

Site of Cistern loft

Residential Chamber

Upper Chamber

Upper Hall

Chapel

level 3

Residential Chambers

Great Reception Chamber Divided in late 13th Century

Residential Chambers

Residential Chambers

0   10m

Trim Castle Site Plan

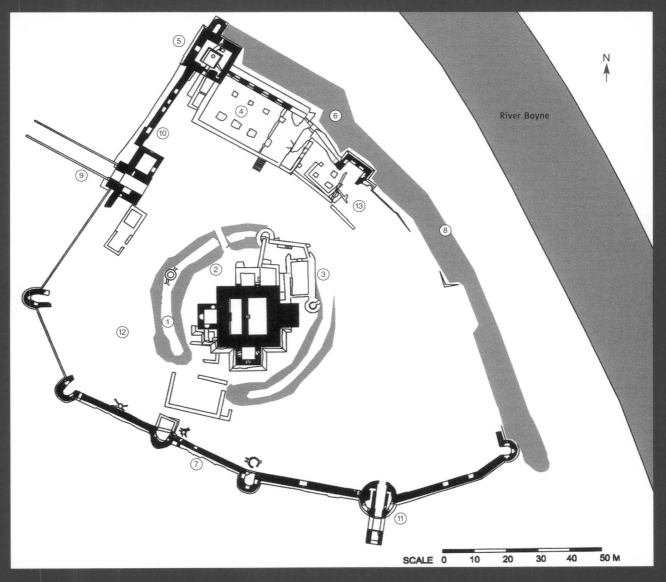

River Boyne

N

SCALE 0   10   20   30   40   50 M

① The Ditch of the Ringwork Castle	⑥ The River Gate	⑪ The Barbican Gate
② The Keep	⑦ The Curtain Walls	⑫ The Bailey
③ The Forebuildings	⑧ The Moat	⑬ The Mint
④ The Great Hall	⑨ The Trim Gate	
⑤ The Solar	⑩ The Prison	

Description of the Castle

THE KEEP or 'Donjon'

Within a castle, the keep was the principal building accommodating the administrative functions of the castle as well as providing domestic privacy and security for the Lord and his family. The keep contained a public hall, great chambers and a chapel as well as quarters for a chaplain, officials and a small garrison, all in one defensible building. Amply stocked cellars ensured that the keep could withstand a long siege, even if the castle yard had been lost. The unique form of the keep at Trim, on the plan of a Greek cross, was an example of the innovative trends in the design of a great noble residence at the end of the 12th century. These variations in design appear to have been aimed principally in achieving improved residential accommodation and orderly communication between rooms within the keep.

Today, views of the ruined Keep are impressive. In the 12th century, the rendered lime-washed facades with its red sandstone dressings, its hoardings and battlements portrayed awesome power.

At Trim, the keep was built in three main phases with many intermediate and later alterations. The subtleties of its geometric layout reveal an intense fervour for symbolism and order. With just tentative breaks with tradition, de Lacy's builders achieved a unique capitol for their master in his new territory. A study of the concept and function of the first structure reveals an intricate system of planning that provided a fitting multi-functional building, a residence and administrative headquarters of a great lord.

The first phase, which could be termed a " hall-keep", was built by Hugh de Lacy in 1175. After Walter's succession in 1194, upper floors were added to the central block, giving the building an elegant appearance, similar to the great towers of many contemporary castle keeps. After 1202, when Walter believed his fortunes lay in Ireland he invested in further developments in Trim Castle. A large open hall was built on a third floor of the central block, followed soon afterwards by the raising of the side towers to their present height.

Description of the Castle

The great stone plinth or 'talus' was built around the base of the keep as a defence against undermining and siege towers. It also allowed stones dropped from the battlements to rebound against attackers. Its value in the circumstances of a siege at such close quarters is questionable and it may been built when the enclosing palisade was removed to give the keep a more elegant appearance.

The keep was built within the enclosure of the original ringwork castle and most of the walls of this first castle were retained to form a private courtyard or ward, as a means of controlling over access to the keep. The gateway to this inner ward was to the north with a drawbridge over a deep ditch. The enclosure was demolished and the ditch was filled in late in the 13th century.

Entry to the keep. The fore-buildings

The enclosure was replaced by a defensive rectangular courtyard, which controlled entry to the keep. The courtyard walls were flanked by three cylindrical towers, of which the footings of two survive. A stone causeway built in the soft filling of the ditch led to the gateway of the courtyard. Inside was a reception hall where the trappings of a long journey were put aside before entering the keep. The main staircase to the door of the keep was built in stone in the narrow passage between the reception hall and the keep. This steep stairway led to the entrance in the east or "Chapel Tower". A drawbridge and an overhanging hoarding once protected this door. Part of the sandstone surround with its bold roll-moulding and drawbar socket survives.

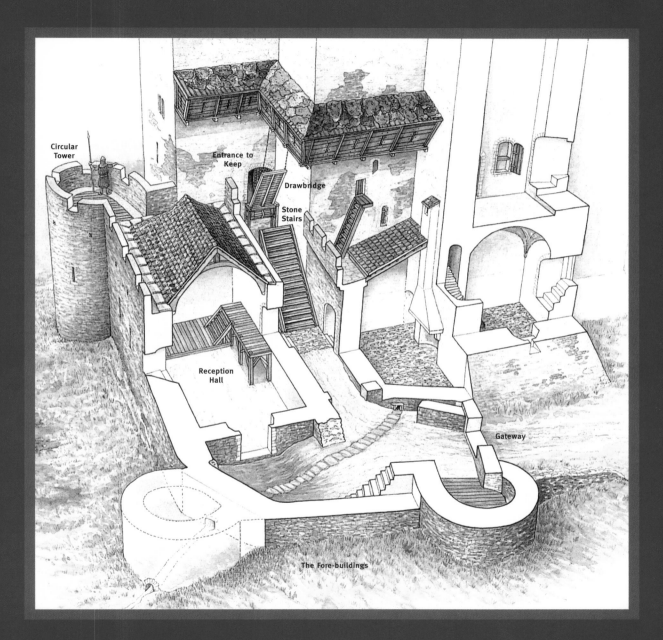

Circular
Tower

Entrance to
Keep

Drawbridge

Stone
Stairs

Reception
Hall

Gateway

The Fore-buildings

Description of the Castle

Level one. The Public rooms of the Main floor

Visitors were received in the vestibule where arms were laid down before passing through two strong doors to the hall. This was the setting for Hugh de Lacy`s court. The main floor of the keep was originally designed as an open arcaded hall. Like the nave of a great abbey, the hall was open from its oak floors to the truss frames of the roof. Beams of light from windows cutting the smoke from a brazier added to the dramatic effect.

However, a parting or dividing wall was inserted early in the construction process, making a permanent division between the hall and chamber. Two stone arches were also inserted in the hall, possibly to support an attic floor within the original roof space.

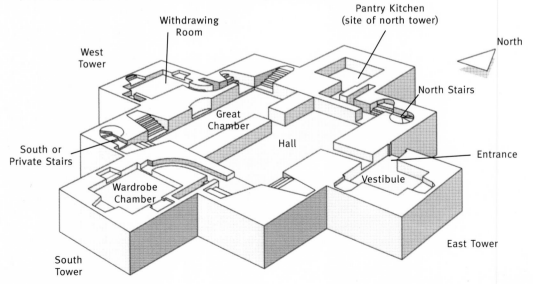

The Hall of Hugh de Lacy's Court

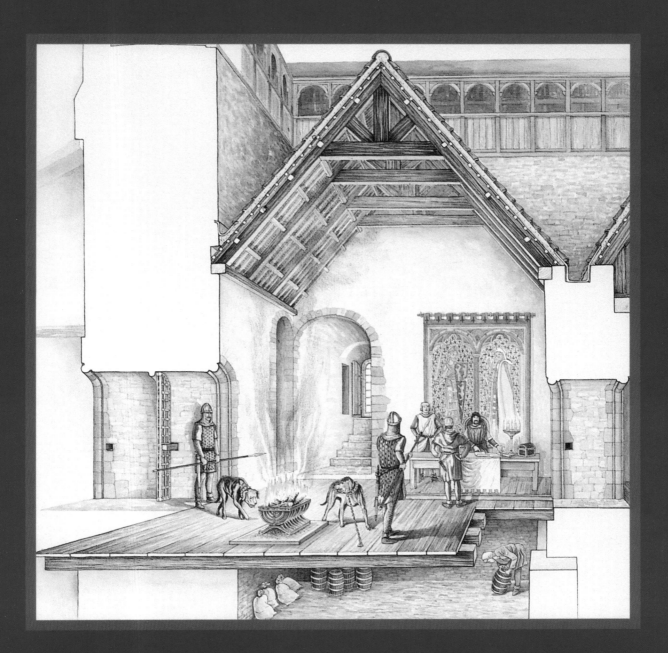

The Fireplace of the Great Chamber

From the kitchen tower to the north, servants brought food from the pantry or from the buttery or larder room below. In the south tower was the "wardrobe chamber" with its cupboard or safe where the ceremonial regalia and documents of the court were kept. In the lower floor is a storage chamber with a cellar below.

It is clear that the defensive aspects of the hall were not forgotten. Steps, from the floor up through the east window, allowed archers quick access to the hoardings. This embrasure was remodelled in the 17th century to make a cannon position. A similar well-preserved stepped embrasure rises from the great chamber and led to a hoarding projecting from the western walls of the keep.

The Private Quarters

From the hall Hugh de Lacy could retreat to his private chambers. This lesser division of the central block is the Great Chamber and was once warmed by a great fireplace, and lit by candles or oil lamps set in recesses in the dividing wall. This was the private dayroom and also a place for council with important guests and officials. Here, the household could spend time together, free of the affairs of their domain. There was a further withdrawing room, complete with latrine (garderobe) in the west tower.

Description of the Castle

The Chapel

A spiral stairway ascends from the hall to the upper floors. A narrow passage leads to the chapel or private oratory. This tall, extraordinarily proportioned room, like the oratories in most castles is situated above the entrance in the east tower. The East window, the Altar stones and the piscina where the altar vessels were washed, are early additions to this room originally built without its chapel furnishings. The fragile stones of the east window now only indicate the form of a three-light glazed window with a fine roll-moulding surround. The southern window may have been similar but in a two light form. The squinting ope of the north window was later adapted to form an access door to a gallery overlooking the main doorway to the castle.

Description of the Castle

The Halls and Chambers of the level 2

From the chapel, a stairway rises to an Upper Hall and Chamber. They are part of the second phase of construction in the 1190's, and were built over the roof space of the first keep. The profiles of the original roofline are visible and the chase of a rain water channel and the bed of a lead water pipe scars the inside of the east wall. The hall is part of the public or administrative division of the keep. It is lit by a large window in the south wall and has a doorway leading to an external gallery or defensive hoarding to the north.

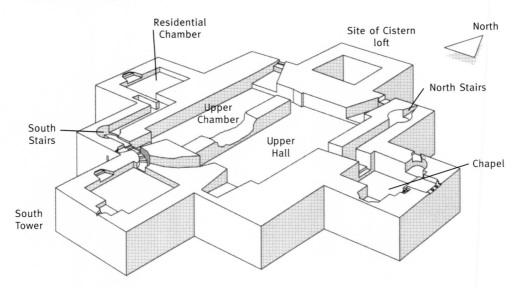

Description of the Castle

A passage, broken through the south wall leads to a remarkable dark chamber, in the south tower in which the original narrow loop windows survive. The absence of a window in the east wall is a departure from the general scheme. This chamber was once linked to the private area and the south stairs. Like the wardrobe chamber below, this room played a part in the public life of the castle. Traces of a lean-to roof, the corbels and rainwater outlet of the original roof can be seen on the walls in this chamber.

From these official rooms the family could retreat to private chambers through the doorway in the parting wall. This chamber is similarly arranged to the upper hall and is part of the private residential division of the keep and may have served as the Ladies' Chamber. Here, the profiles of the roofs of the first keep can be seen as a scar on the inner face of the stonework of the north and south walls.

From these floors there is no access to the north tower where a loft housed the rainwater cisterns, which supplied the kitchen below. Over the Upper Hall and Chamber narrow passageways linked the stairs with attic or galleries. There are no marks of the second phase roofs on the masonry, though they were set below the wall-walk level. However fragments of the roof timbers are preserved on the dividing wall.

Description of the Castle

The Residential Chamber

From the south stairs, a passage leads
to the principal Residential Chamber in
the west tower. The additional comforts
and improvements made to this chamber
distinguish it from other chambers in the
keep. A remarkable feature of the early
work is the replacement of the lean-to
roof with a cruck framed or curved truss
roof. The roof truss now modelled in its
settings gave this room status and
grandeur. The north window ope was
adapted to make a fireplace, and later a
two-light ogee-headed window replaced
the simple stone dressings of the west
window. Outside, the cleaning house
was built on to provide a latrine and
washroom. Access to the garderobe
tower was blocked up in the 15th
century when the tower had collapsed or
was demolished. There is a small mural
garderobe off the passage between the
residential chamber and
the stairs.

Description of the Castle

The Upper Floors

By 1200, and within a few years of the beginning of Walter de Lacy`s tenure, a further major redevelopment of the keep was undertaken. These works added a great open hall on a third floor of the keep. Unlike the 'Hall of de Lacy's Court' on the main floor this was a place of great ceremony. To be received by the Lord of Meath was the privilege of only the closest and trusted of his companions. This development of the keep, therefore, has closer affinities with a great solar chamber built for the private use of the household rather than the public hall of a medieval court.

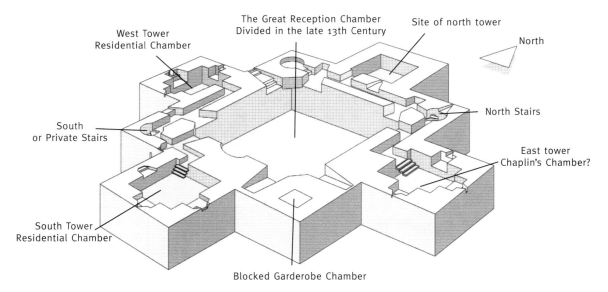

West Tower
Residential Chamber

The Great Reception Chamber
Divided in the late 13th Century

Site of north tower

North

North Stairs

South
or Private Stairs

East tower
Chaplin's Chamber?

South Tower
Residential Chamber

Blocked Garderobe Chamber

Description of the Castle

Entry to this upper floor was from a wooden gallery along the west wall, from a short balcony off of the north stairs. The former attic passages below the galleries were adapted as service passages at floor level. A fireplace in the south wall, with its dressed red sandstone surround, heated the hall. This large square area may have been covered in the familiar form of the double hip roof, requiring a framework of wooden arcading as support under a central valley. The walls of the central tower were raised between the existing cap-houses with new cap-houses built above them. These walls were built as vaulted mural passages, and with the galleries, allowed full circulation within the upper keep. From the mural passages overlooking the side towers the occupants had unrestricted views of the surrounding countryside.

Within a short period of time, the side towers were raised to their present height. They accommodated new upper chambers off the passages of the gallery level. In the west tower the room is furnished with a fine corner fireplace. Two of the loops are the original unglazed shuttered windows while the west window was later rebuilt in the late 12th century to form a simple sandstone two light glazed ope.

Description of the Castle

A 19th century illustration shows the upper floor divided by a third tier of the parting wall. Two stone pointed arches span the eastern division and appear to be supports, like stone trusses, for the roof. It is not clear how the new layout relates to the fireplace. Dean Butler recorded the collapse of the arches in 1820. The great fall of stones brought the upper parting wall down, but no mark exists, for, as with the lower parting wall, it was not bonded to the casing walls of the keep.

No fixed date for the building of the third tier of the parting wall can be suggested, but it may have occurred in the context of the building a new Great Hall on the site of the north curtain wall. Movable screens or partitions allowed the floors to be further divided, as events required.

The southern chamber has a latrine outlet in the bay of the east window. Here, two windows were enlarged while the south window survives as a loop. A blocked loop in the abutting walls of the central tower is a surviving remnant of the passage leading to the latrine in the southeast corner. The plan is continued in the eastern chamber, though here, the south ope was demolished and rebuilt as a fireplace as late as the 16th century. A loop, once lighting the blocked mural gallery, can also be traced here and seen in original form where a loop lights the north section of the mural gallery. We must assume that the missing northern chamber followed the usual plan.

The Interior of Trim Castle drawn by T.B. Godwin for "The Excursions to Ireland" 1819.

Description of the Castle

The Roof and Wall-Walks

Four turrets or cap-houses surmount the walls of the keep. Two cover the spiral stairways.
The southeast cap-house is a garderobe chamber, while the northwest is a simple chamber for the comfort of the defenders on watch. Between the turrets, the wall-walks were covered in a wooden structure called an "alure" and were linked by angled or "squinch" landings at each corner.

A twin-hipped roof with a central valley covered the keep. Like the earlier roofs, it was formed to allow for the collection of rainwater, which could be stored in barrels for when it was required. Red clay roof tiles completed the roof. These tiles were shaped to interlock and, unlike the tiles of southern Europe, they were made with a clay hook to allow them to be fixed to the steep pitched roof structure.

The Garderobe Tower in the SW Corner

The excavations of 1971-4 revealed the footings of a tower enclosing the garderobes outlets. This was linked to the 1st and 2nd level residential chambers of the west tower. Doors, now blocked, were made in the window opes in the south wall of the tower. It is not easy to date the garderobe tower, but it was already built when the plinth was added to the base of the keep before 1200. A history of phased construction is indicated where the lower walls abut the keep and the upper walls are outlined only by the scar where this tower was bonded with the keep. The collapse or at least the abandonment of the garderobe tower took place in the later Middle Ages.

Corbeling under a Cap-House

Scar of Lean-to Roof

Line of Waterpipe

Put Log Hole

Wash House Extension

Serving Passage to Pantry

Stone-vaulted Ceiling

Description of the Castle

Looking at The North Tower

The collapsed north tower gives a sectional view of the arrangement of this, the service or kitchen tower. The foundations were uncovered during the 1995 archaeological excavations. The chamber at ground floor level, of which remnants of a stone vaulted ceiling remain, served as a cold store or larder. An original wooden floor was suspended almost 2 metres above the modern ground level. The floor level was lowered in the 14th century and a paved floor and a door was cut through under the stair to a "wash-house" extension. Access to the main floor was through the narrow mural stair, connecting with the passage between pantry or " little kitchen" and the hall. The pantry is on the main floor level and is connected to the hall by a wide serving passage. The valuable serving plate was kept in a cupboard with a red sandstone surround. This room was open to a cistern loft above, where a scar like a row of pigeon holes mark the line of a pipe that once carried rain water to the cisterns. Traces of the early lean-to roof are visible, here some details are different from the early roof of the other towers. The inserted covering course of stones and the lower supporting corbels suggest that this tower was initially roofed below the level of the lean-to roof. The upper floor was part of the latest development of the keep. It was reached only from the upper mural passage and linked to all upper floors, suggesting its use was for that of the household and officials.

External Features of the Keep

Timbers
The walls of the keep are perforated by three horizontal rows of putlog holes (p.48). The lowest row is the sockets of principal supporting timbers of a defensive hoarding dating to the mid-1170's. The middle row provided four wood samples for scientific dating. These formed part of the scaffolding framework of Hugh de Lacy's builders in the years before 1180. The upper row offered evidence for two further developments of the Keep.

Description of the Castle

The samples taken from the walls of the central block were part of the supports of the second hoarding of 1196. It encircled the central block above the lean-to roofs of the side towers. The wood samples taken from the side towers were the remains of rough unworked timbers and completed the scaffolding when these towers were raised soon after 1202.

Windows

Many of the original loop windows survive and date from the 1170's to the early years of the 13th century. Some were enlarged in later years and two were adapted to make fireplaces. The east window in the chapel is an early replacement of a loop. In the west tower a 15th century twin light ogee headed window lights the residential chamber but now without its central mullion. A window of twin rectangular lights replaced the west-facing loop of the upper chamber and may be the only survivor of a series of windows lighting the upper level of the keep.

Fragments of the carved stone allow some appreciation of the elegance of the windows that once lit the hall and chamber of the main floor. The "transitional style" of tall round headed window embrasures is used with the low segmental arches of the doorways.

The large opes of the windows of the second level replaced the unglazed loops that once lit and ventilated the roof space of the first keep. The proportions of the openings are similar to the windows of the Great Hall and may have been of a comparable design and part de Geneville's renewal of the castle in the late 13th century.

The Great Hall

Throughout the Middle Ages, The Great Hall was the principal building of many great stone castles. For centuries it was a symbol of the great power, wealth and hospitality of the resident Lord and was the focus of medieval secular life. This was the place of assembly for the lord and his tenants where courts and the administration of the lordship were conducted and ceremonial gatherings, as well as feasts and celebrations were held. Built in the latter half of the 13th century, the Great Hall at Trim superseded the hall within the keep. It was constructed utilising the northeast section of the curtain wall alongside the river. This provided a relatively safe position by affording shelter from projectiles that had become a feature of increasingly sophisticated methods of siege warfare. On the riverfront, the curtain wall was raised in height, the lower earlier defensive openings in the walls were blocked up and the ground inside was raised to form a sub-floor. The surrounds of four of the five large windows that once lit the hall can be seen, although these were subsequently blocked up by one of the garrisons of the Confederate wars in the 1640's. There would have been similar large windows in the west wall.

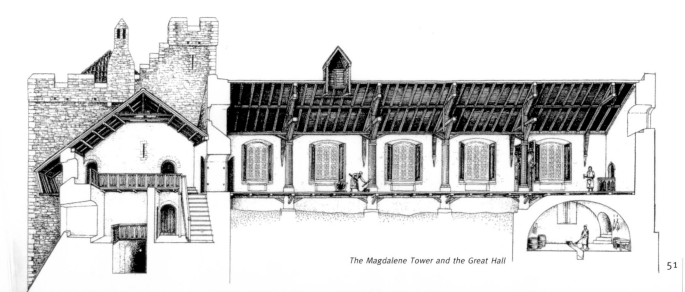

The Magdalene Tower and the Great Hall

51

Description of the Castle

The Great Hall at Trim Castle conformed to the usual medieval arrangement, with a dais or platform for the Lord's table near the doorway to the solar. At the opposite end was the service area where a screen passage separated the hall from the buttery and pantry. There was an open fire, usually placed on a central axis about two thirds of the way along from the lower end. A high roof, surmounted with a lantern-like open louvre, allowed smoke to escape. The kitchen or pantry and the larder cellar of the Hall were situated at the southern end of this range of buildings.

In 1367, Edward III, ordered that new building works be carried out at Trim Castle, including the enlargement of the hall. Orders were given

> 'To rebuild...the chambers of the red hall beneath the said castle which
> Are joined to the tower called Magdalene Tower in that castle, and the
> Chambers joined to this same tower, including walls, wooden planks,
> Iron, lead, and all other necessary roofing.'

This was to be carried out prior to the return of his estates to Edmund Mortimer, 3rd Earl of March, who was to be married in 1368, to the king's granddaughter, Philippa. Built on the same site, the new hall was much wider than the earlier one. The line of the previous west wall can be traced from the inner row of piers whose bases may still be seen in the ground. Ornate oak columns rising from stone bases were used to support the large central span of the roof when aisles were created to either side.

Originally the Great Hall had a suspended wooden floor above the cellars, with a door in the south wall leading to the river gate. Later, a stone vault was inserted in the undercroft. The river entrance was closed and the rock-cut passage from the river was filled in. At ground level above the passageway an extension was built, possibly to serve as a kitchen. A new entrance and step-way to the castle yard was made in the east wall possibly close to the principal doorway. This range of buildings was further extended early in the 15th century. Excavations have uncovered the wall and pier footings of a second aisled building to the south of the Great Hall. This hall or barn was awkwardly aligned, as if it was squeezed between the Great Hall and the curtain wall. By 1460 this building was replaced by the metal-workshops of the Mint.

At Trim, seven parliaments were held in the 15th century and it is likely that some were held in the Great Hall. Among the usual acts relating to revenues, property and crime were those designed to preserve the identity of the inhabitants of the "Pale". In 1447, an Act forbade an Englishman to wear a *"beard upon his upper lips alone"*. Dress code also occupied much of the parliament's time in 1465, when Irishmen were ordered to go *"apparelled"* like Englishmen, and that they should take surnames of a town, a trade or a colour.

The Cellar of the Great Hall

Description of the Castle

The Solar or " Magdalene Tower"

The northwest Tower was certainly the strongest and probably the earliest, of the curtain wall towers. The blocked arrow loops visible in the external walls are a feature of its early defensive nature. Situated close to the river, it would have guarded the ford, which was a major crossing point on the River Boyne. In many castles in the 13th century the "palace range" with accommodation towers situated adjacent to the great hall replaced the apartments in the keep as the residence of the lord and his family.

Adjoining the Great Hall the Magdalene Tower was enlarged and reconstructed to provide more comfortable lodgings. It may originally have had three storeys above a cellar. The topmost level in the form of a garret contained the solar or living quarters but no longer survives. Beneath the solar was a private day room to which the lord and lady withdrew from the Great Hall. On the first floor was the private reception room with a doorway to a gallery overlooking the river, possibly with a stairway leading to the harbour. A spiral stair in the south-west corner linked the middle floors with mural stairs continuing to the upper floor. Fireplaces were installed in the large rooms on the upper two floors and there was a large window inserted in the river wall on the second floor. The necessities of life were provided for when a latrine tower, projecting from the principal rooms, was built over the moat. At the western end of Great Hall a porch provided a sheltered passageway between the hall and the living quarters in the "Magdalene Tower"

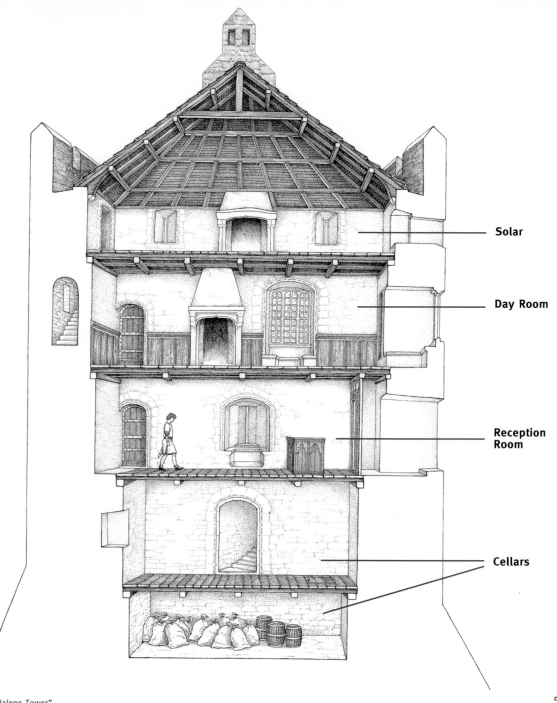

Solar

Day Room

Reception
Room

Cellars

The Solar or "Magdalene Tower"

Description of the Castle

The River Gate. Navigating the Boyne

The river gate and harbour at Trim Castle is at the end of an extensive system of river navigation that once operated along the River Boyne. This feat of engineering enabled the delivery of stores by boat from the port of Drogheda. The medieval navigation of the river is yet to be studied, but would have involved the cutting of short stretches of canal that bypassed the natural falls in the river. The water levels were controlled by a system of weirs and locks. A short distance from the castle, a dry and partly infilled section of canal with a ruined stone bridge survives along the north bank at a section of the river known as the Maudlins. A section of the moat was widened to form a small harbour situated below the Great Hall. Boats could be moored in the harbour and supplies and traded goods delivered through the River Gate, made in the eastern side of the curtain wall to the south of the Great Hall. Inside the River Gate, a passage was cut through the bedrock to the door of the cellars. The maintenance of a river transport system on the Boyne was difficult to sustain and was abandoned before 1400. The River Gate and doorway were blocked, the passage was back filled and an extension to the hall was built on the site.

The Moat

Description of the Castle

The Moat

The River Boyne was channelled to form an essential part of the first line of defence of the castle. The moat which washed the curtain walls was fed and controlled by a system of weirs and sluices on the Boyne. The digging of the moat was also a source of rock for the builders of the castle. The southern curtain walls are set on higher ground, and here a small tributary river called the 'Leper River' was diverted to fill this section of the moat. The weirs were a persistent source of conflict, as valuable fishing rights were disputed in the courts of the castle. These weirs are listed among the possessions of the monasteries of Trim in 1536 when they were no longer of any usefulness to the castle and its neglected moat.

Boatmen from Topographia Hiberniae
Giraldus Cambrensis 1189.

The Curtain Walls

By 1180, once the keep had been made secure, the builders set about replacing the external timber defences with stone walls strengthened by towers. Available evidence suggests that the towers were built first and sections of wall were inserted into the gaps. During construction, the quarrying of stone, particularly in the northern section created natural escarpments. On the northwest aspect, a section of wall, from the Trim gate to the Magdalene tower presented the most formidable aspect of the outer defences with the walls looming almost eight metres above the moat. The walls along the riverfront were laid out at the same time. Here they closely follow the contours of the hill and incorporate the defensive advantages of the river.

There were at least two main phases of construction. Walls to the north and along the river were constructed before the southern sections. The later walls were built to greater height and further heightened at a later date. The lower tier of archers' loops, present in the first phase, was not included in the southern walls.

The Curtain Walls and Barbican Gate.

Description of the Castle

Two large fortified gatehouses formed part of the outer walled defences. There was also the watergate on the river side, and two small gates or "sallyports", often used for concealed access to the castle, but which also allowed the defenders to counter-attack a besieging force.

Square flanking towers were a feature of the earlier riverside walls of the enclosure. However, the design of the later flanking towers of the south curtain walls was changed into the open-backed D-shaped towers. These were more resistant to battering from projectiles and were more difficult to undermine. These later rounded towers serve as examples of changes that were taking place in siege warfare during the period from the end of the 12th to the beginning of 13th centuries.

Early sieges were mainly passive, in that attacking armies simply blockaded the castle or town. The introduction of siege machines led to more aggressive forms of attack, and, in turn, to stronger defences. Improved defensive measures included the increased height of the walls, with arrow loops concentrated in the towers creating a 'killing ground' below the walls. An even more effective array of loops was introduced in the Barbican Gate. Wooden hoardings projecting from the upper walls provided shelter for the garrison attacking 'sappers' attempting to breach the base of walls and towers. Generally, access to wall walks was from the various towers, particularly the gate towers, although ladders were also used. In the tower to the east of the Barbican Gate, the direct access to the wall-walk can still be seen where a (now blocked) mural staircase opened onto that section of the wall-walk.

The battlements or crenellations of the walls do not survive. They were deliberately removed by the royalist garrison before abandoning the castle to the army of Oliver Cromwell in 1649.

Description of the Castle

The Trim Gate

The Trim Gate is so called because it became enveloped in the town that grew in its shelter. It was the earliest and probably the only gate of Trim Castle until the 'Barbican Gate' was completed. Located close to the crossing on the River Boyne, it was built on the site of an earlier timber gatehouse, dating from 1172, which had formed part of the original wooden outer encircling palisade.

The stone gatehouse constructed around 1180 forms the core of the present gate. This was a simple rectangular structure of two storeys, projecting outwards from the curtain walls. Approach to it was by a steep ramp leading to a retractable 'drawbridge'. The drawbridge was protected within a 'barbican', but only fragments of the parapet walls survive where they were bonded to the gate tower. Under the semi-circular gate arch are the vertical grooves and the retracting slot of the portcullis, a strong grille of wood and iron that protected the gate. An external stair on the southern wall leads to the upper floor. A wooden floor built above the passageway provided a platform for soldiers to observe traffic passing below. This floor housed the windlass and pulleys that lifted the portcullis. A 'murder hole' in the archway, blocked during later reconstruction, protected the gates from battering and attempts to burn the gate could be drenched with water.

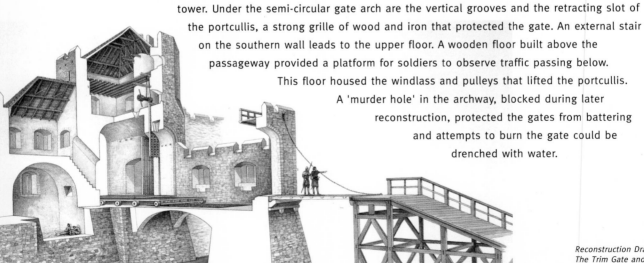

Reconstruction Drawing of The Trim Gate and Prison in the 13th Century

Description of the Castle

Early in the 13th century the gatehouse was reconstructed, probably as repairs following the siege of 1224. A stone barrel vault pierced by a 'murder hole' replaced the wooden floor over the passage and the lifting mechanism for the portcullis was repositioned in the chamber above the vault. Porters' or constables' lodgings were situated in new rooms on the upper floor. A spiral staircase linked the upper rooms and continued to the wall-walks at roof level. The upper floors of the gate tower were rebuilt to a semi-octagonal plan leaving a chamfered or an angular outer façade. This is reminiscent of work in other de Lacy castles but here it is a reconstruction, and may have been built to strengthen the tower against projectiles.

The Prison.

The prison block constructed against the north east walls of the gatehouse were the last buildings in this range and may date to the late 13th century. It contained a vaulted room with its floor level set well below the ground of the castle yard. This served as the prison cell, with guardroom accommodation above. Access to the roof level was via an external stair tower built over the wall-walks and garderobe chamber at the end of the northwestern section curtain wall.

Surviving accounts detail salaries paid to constables and watchmen in the 14th century. In 1362, a commission inquired into the suspicious death in custody of Art MacMurrough, King of Leinster, and his deputy in the prison of Trim Castle. Other accounts describe the harsh overcrowded conditions of prisoners in manacles. Constables were also taken to task for allowing prisoners to escape.

The Trim Gate from the Bailey

Description of the Castle

The Barbican Gate

The second of two principal gates at Trim Castle, the Barbican Gate, was constructed during the early years of the 13th century after the curtain wall had been completed. It is an elegant blend of forms. The tall cylindrical tower, and the rectangular outer tower are cut through by pointed (gothic) arches, while the round arches of the 'barbican" bridge link both towers. The design was more sophisticated than that of the earlier Trim Gate as new ideas that had been developed abroad, were also being applied in Ireland.

The "Barbican Gate" was built as a single tower that straddles the entrance passage instead of the twin circular towers more commonly found in Ireland. The gatehouse was defended by a 'barbican', the outer defences of a forward tower and bridge. Defensive firepower was maximised from an array of 'arrow slits' in both towers. Above the gate passage of the gatehouse, there were another two storeys. Internally, they are polygonal in shape and are accessed by a spiral stair that ascends from the passageway. The windlass or lifting mechanism was housed on the first floor while comfortable lodgings for officials were created on the upper floor. The remains of fireplaces and a latrine chamber can still be seen. The upper section of the gate tower was completed with battlements, reached from the turret that capped the stair well.

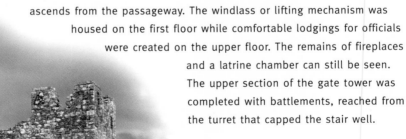

Description of the Castle

Entry to the castle was a progress through a series of controlled compartments. An elaborate system of bridges, gates, overhead traps and observation loops was designed to allow the garrison total control over access. At the end of a steep ramp the obstacles of the outer tower were encountered. While being watched from the upper floor of this tower, those seeking entrance crossed a pit before reaching the draw-bridge. Beyond the bridge was the tall gate tower, strongly defended by a portcullis with a heavy wooden gate blocking entrance to the central passage. In turn, flanking guardrooms protected the passage and there was another wooden gate before entry to the castle yard. The segmental vault has collapsed. It may have been pierced by a series of parallel 'murder slots' overlooking the passage between the portcullis and the inner gate. While the gate arches are unadorned, the portcullis groove is defined in carved red sandstone. The axle socket or pivot of the draw-bridge is set off centre of the crown of the supporting arches. The bridge may have been operated from a gallery above the bridge, as there are no lifting chain slots in the gate tower.

Description of the Castle

The Bailey

The Buildings and Activities in the Castle Yard.

The walls of the castle enclose an area of 1.5 hectares and, apart from the inner enclosure, appear not to have been divided into wards. The areas that have been excavated show that the demand on space was great and mostly used by the garrison and servants and the many trades and craft-workers required in the maintenance of the castle. The open space available would have been laid out into work yards and assembly areas with spaces for animal pens. Small garden plots produced vegetables, cooking and medicinal herbs, and plants and berries grown for textile colouring. Medieval castle gardens were formally laid out as a place of relaxation for the family. The keeping of poultry, rabbits, bees and pigeons was common in castle grounds. The "castle orchard" and a dovecot are recorded as being in the custody of Thomas Broun in 1425, though they may have been outside the walls.

Work on renovating the castle buildings was ongoing. Lime kilns, producing lime for building mortar and plaster, date from the 12th to the 17th century. Even the towers of the fore-buildings

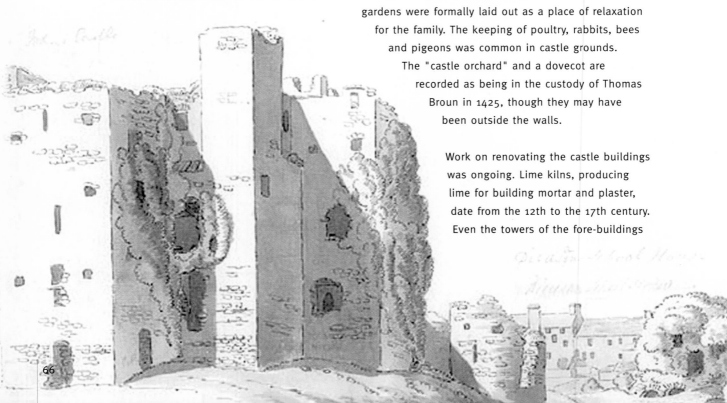

were adapted for use as kilns after they fell into disuse. In the 14th century, building work necessitated the quarrying of stone from within the bailey. Flooding of the quarry prompted the building of a stone lined cistern or well with inlet and overflow gullies as the quarry refilled. Many of the buildings within the bailey were concentrated to the south of the Great Hall. They served as kitchens, bake-houses and smithies or armourers' workshops. Possibly at this furnace the metals were mixed for the minting of coins. The Mint, which was built on the site of an aisled building, like a small version of the hall, was possibly a temporary structure, awkwardly fitted between the southern end of the Great Hall and the curtain wall.

Houses, stables and barns were commonly built against the curtain wall, often as timbered framed structures. Adjoining the Barbican Gate are the remains of a substantial house built in stone. This was more than a simple lean-to construction, the inner wall of this house, built against the curtain wall, contained fireplaces at two floors. Inside the Trim Gate the footings of a 14th century house were discovered, built on the bank of clay deposited here by the quarry workers. This modest freestanding residence comprised a first floor over stores or an animal shelter at ground level. In 1610, Sir James Carroll was granted the manor of Trim on condition that he built a *'competent and convenient house'* and a good and safe county gaol upon the site of the ruinous castle of Trim. It is unclear if this project was proceeded with, though rebels led by Myles O'Reilly burned a house adjoining Trim Castle in 1641.

The Keep looking towards the Mint Tower,
Daniel Grose, 1791.
Courtesy: National Library of Ireland.

Description of the Castle

The Mint.

The curtain wall tower overlooking the river has been called the "Mint tower" for many generations. When the area inside this tower was excavated the remains of a series of buildings periodically destroyed and replaced was uncovered. Layers of ash and burnt surfaces and spills of molten copper indicate the use of these buildings as small metal-workshops but the manufacture of coins on this site remains unproven.

In 1460, following Richard of York's (Lieutenant of Ireland) failure to capture the throne, he retreated to Ireland. He called a parliament at Drogheda to rally the support of the Anglo-Irish community. The parliament provided for the issuing of distinctive coinage to be minted in the castles of Dublin and Trim. The Act stipulated the weight and content of the coins; such as the copper coin "The Patrick" having a cross on one side with inscription Salvator. On the other side is the image of a Bishop with the dedication Patricius. Also described in the Act is a silver penny the Irlandes d'argent imprinted with a crown and a cross.

These Irish coins were struck to ease a decline in circulation of coinage caused by the 'decay of trade' and to help finance Richard's ambitions. However by December Richard was killed at Wakefield and only after the victory at the battle of Towton in March 1461, was Richard's son, Edward, proclaimed king.

As Edward IV, he appointed Christopher Fox comptroller of the mints at Dublin and Trim and two years later, Germyn Lynch was appointed *'warden and master worker of monies and coignes'*. After 1471, the mint operated only in Dublin castle but in 1478 the striking of all manner of coins of silver was permitted within the castle of Trim. The existence of a mint at Trim required a sophisticated system of accounting as well as skills in the preparation of consistent metals and their weights and measures. A smelting workshop would only be part of the manufacture of coins. A secure place within the castle was also required to control and store the coins, moulds, punches and precious metals. Offices to keep accounts and organise distribution would also have formed part of the mint.

The Town Walls

The walls of Trim enclose 28 hectares divided by the Boyne. The walls run in long continuous stretches, and were watched over by towers at each corner and above the gates. Only the fragments of one of these towers can be traced. The two districts are linked near the ancient fording place. A bridge is first recorded in 1194 and again when the "new bridge" burned in 1203. The existing bridge was built to replace a stone bridge destroyed in a flood in 1330.

The focus of the early ecclesiastical settlement at Trim was on the north bank of the River Boyne. The southern bank (the site of the castle) was not intensively settled but may have formed a peripheral part of the emerging town. There are no remains of pre-Norman defences. They would have comprised a strong enclosing wall or earthen bank and ditch following the contours around the high ground although the outline of the early settlement may be reflected in the curve of High Street.

Throughout the 13th century the districts were almost equal in area, but by the end of the 14th century the borough had expanded to the north and enclosed the grounds of St. Mary's Abbey. To the south of the Dublin Gate, a medieval suburb developed and was protected within earthen ramparts. Outside the Navan Gate, the "Greek Park" believed to be the site of an ancient church and school was also enclosed as a suburb but appears not to have been divided into burgage plots.

The development of the town may be traced in the murage charters. The first, dating to 1289, was granted for seven years for enclosing *'the vill and the greater security of Ireland'*. A second charter in 1316 may have been aimed at strengthening the defences of Trim during the Scottish invasion under Edward Bruce. No details of this charter are available. Generally in murage charters, tolls, customs on livestock and traded goods, were documented and Fair days are usually stipulated, usually set on a Saint's day. The revenues met the cost of building and maintaining the walls and the protection of the walls made the town a safe and orderly place in which commerce could thrive.

The Town Walls

By the end of the 14th century most of Ireland was governed by the Gaelic families or the "Gaelicised" Norman magnates. Trim was at the frontier of the territory obedient to the Crown. In 1393, Roger Mortimer (5th Earl) had for twenty years licence to appoint collectors of certain tolls and customs of all goods sold in the town of Trim. The revenues were to be used to surround the town with a stone wall, paving and improving the town and repressing the adjacent enemies. Most of the surviving town defences and the gate are vestiges of this period. In 1423 this grant was renewed and ascribes greater importance to Trim as the focus of order and security in Meath.

The only surviving gate, The "Sheep Gate", stands isolated as it straddles the medieval road across the Porch Field from Newtown. Other gates carried the name of the town beyond such as the Athboy and Navan Gates. Today, the names only survive as areas within the town of Trim. A sixth gate may have stood on the west wall at the end of a lane running through the town from St Mary's Abbey.

Documentary evidence leaves the closure of each circuit of the walls undefined along the riverfronts. It seems likely that the walls closed the southern circuit along the riverside, if only to provide flood protection on the southern bank. The Water Gate and a possible "Bridge Gate" referred to in 1689 may be part of a river front wall.

Rev. Robert Draper when writing to Lord Burghley in 1584 proposing a university in Trim, boasted, *"the town in the midst of the English Pale is strongly walled and would be of great safety to the whole company of students there."* At the time of the Confederate wars (1642) the accounts of the condition of the walls are far less favourable *"so old and ruinous as afforded in some places of it entrance to horse".*

In the latter years of the 17th century the corporation of Trim ordered the walls and gates to be inspected. Money was provided for repairs to the Navan Gate and to supply the guard with a fire and candle during the winter months. In 1689, the inhabitants of Trim were required to do six days' work repairing the walls on the south side of the corporation. The bridge gate (Trim Gate) and the

The Town Walls

drawbridge gate of the castle were to be repaired and the *"back doors"* in the walls to be closed up.

Along its south and west lengths, the wall is well preserved, but the battlements and wall-walks do not survive. It is substantially built and stands 2.5 metres above the modern ground level and is 1.4m in width. Recent excavations along the southern stretch revealed sections of the wall with a wide outer ditch, once filled by the Leper River. The eastern stretch around the Sheep Gate, which enclosed the precinct of the abbey, is less substantial but its line is well preserved. Within the walls the outline of the medieval garden plots have been largely retained in the property boundaries of the modern town.

The Water Gate photographed by Jane Shackleton in 1889.

Courtesy: Royal Society of Antiquaries of Ireland